Witness History Series

THE ARAB-ISRAELI CONFLICT

Paul Harper

The Bookwright Press
New York · 1990

Titles in this series

The Arab–Israeli Conflict
China since 1945
The Cold War
The Origins of World War I
The Russian Revolution
South Africa since 1948
The Third Reich
The United Nations
The United States since 1945

Cover illustration: Arab women and Israeli soldiers share the sidewalk in the small town of Khan Yunis, in the Gaza Strip.

First published in the
United States in 1990 by
The Bookwright Press
387 Park Avenue South
New York, NY 10016

First published in 1989 by
Wayland (Publishers) Ltd
61 Western Road, Hove
East Sussex BN3 1JD

Library of Congress Cataloging-in-Publication Data
Harper, Paul, 1944–
    The Arab–Israeli conflict/by Paul Harper
        p. cm. – (Witness history)
    Bibliography: p.
    Includes index.
    Summary: A history of conflict in the Middle East, which has
raged for most of the twentieth century.

    ISBN 0-531-18294-0
    1. Jewish–Arab relations – Juvenile literature. [1. Jewish–Arab
relations.] I. Title. II. Series
DS119.7.H3763   1990
956–dc20   89–7036
                                                        CIP
                                                         AC

Typeset by Kalligraphics Limited, Horley, Surrey
Printed by Sagdos, S.p.A., Milan

Contents

1
THE ROOTS OF VIOLENCE
East meets West 1900–17

IN HISTORICAL TERMS, THE political map of the whole of the Middle East with its patchwork of rival, sometimes warring, states is a recent creation. One hundred years ago a map would have shown the area all colored the same: the heartlands of the Muslim Empire ruled by the Turkish Ottoman dynasty. An average citizen of the Empire would probably not have thought of himself as a Syrian or a Palestinian, or even necessarily as an Arab, but simply as a Muslim subject of the Sultan in Istanbul.

By the start of this century, however, the Ottoman Empire, having ruled most of the Arab world for some 400 years, was on the verge of collapse. Compared with the powerful, industrialized nations of neighboring Europe, the Empire was hopelessly backward and underdeveloped. Eager to expand their military and economic power further, the European states – principally Britain, France, Germany and Russia – eyed these vast strategic territories of the Ottoman Empire hungrily. Britain was particularly

The Ottoman Empire in 1912, just before its destruction during World War I. It was the last of the great Islamic empires.

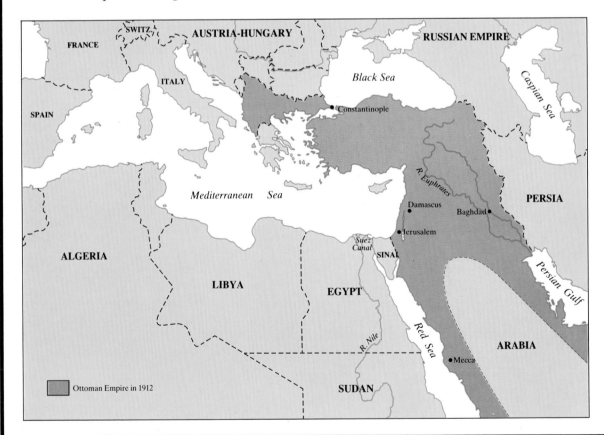

Ottoman Empire in 1912

4

▲ Kaiser Wilhelm II in Palestine in 1898. The Turks' alliance with Germany in World War I led the Allied Powers to attack the Ottoman Empire.

◄ Colonel T. E. Lawrence, a leading figure in the British-backed Arab revolt against the Ottoman Turks in 1916.

anxious for more influence in the region, because the Middle East lay directly across the route to its prize imperial possession, India. Russian expansion southward into the Middle East was Britain's greatest fear.

The Ottoman Empire was also threatened from within by the first stirrings of Arab nationalism – a force that was to be exploited by Britain in the scramble among the European nations to seize territory when the Ottoman Empire finally collapsed. The Sultan's alliance with Germany in World War I (1914–18) made Britain and France allies against the Turkish forces in the Middle East. The British realized that an Arab uprising against the Turks would be a great help to their own war effort, and began looking around for a suitable Arab to lead such a revolt. They came up with Hussein ibn Ali, ruler of the Muslim holy city of Mecca. The Arab Revolt duly began in June 1916, backed by British arms and military advisers. Hussein was persuaded to side with a foreign Christian power against the Muslim Turks by the promise of Arab independence in

all of what is now Syria, Lebanon, Jordan, Israel and Iraq. In fact, at the same time that Britain was negotiating with Hussein about the future of the post-Ottoman Middle East, it was secretly doing the same thing with its wartime allies France and Russia. An agreement was reached in May 1916 to divide up the area into zones of French and British control. The Sykes-Picot Agreement, as it was known after its British and French negotiators, was followed by what the Arabs regarded as another betrayal by Britain of the promise of their independence. On November 2, 1917, about a month before British troops captured Jerusalem from the Turks, Britain's foreign secretary, Arthur James Balfour, wrote a letter to a leading British Jew, Lord Rothschild. The letter, which was to change the history of the Middle East, began:

His Majesty's Government view with favor the establishment in Palestine of a national home for the Jewish people, and will use their best endeavors to facilitate the achievement of this object . . .[1]

The Middle East mosaic

By the end of World War I, the occupation of the Arab world by the European powers was complete, except for a few remote, thinly populated areas. The vast majority of the Arabs were Muslims. Islam in fact is the religion of the Arabs in a special sense. Its founder, the Prophet Muhammad, was an Arab born in Mecca in the seventh century AD. Under the banner of the new religion, the tribes of the Arabian Peninsula conquered the Middle East and North Africa, converting their original peoples as they went. The Muslims captured Palestine in the seventh century AD. In adopting the religion, language and culture of their conquerors, the original Palestinians

The Arabian Commission to the Paris peace conference in 1919, including Lawrence of Arabia. Their appeal for Arab independence was ignored by the victorious Allies.

became Arabs themselves, though racially they were a mixture of many other peoples as well, among them Romans, Greeks, Jews, and Crusaders from Europe. The capital of Palestine, Jerusalem, has always had a special significance for Muslims, who believe that the Prophet Muhammad ascended to heaven from there in AD 619.

The Middle East was not wholly peopled by Muslims, however. There were important Christian and Jewish communities in most of the major towns and cities outside of the Arabian peninsula, as well as other sects and offshoots from the three main religions. Under the old Ottoman system, such minorities officially enjoyed a separate, protected status. Despite the prejudices and the inequalities that existed in reality, the system did actually prevent the kind of religious persecution long suffered by Jews in Europe, for instance. Friction between the different sectarian groups in the Middle East first arose as a serious problem in the nineteenth century as a consequence of the European penetration of the area. The European powers took the local Christians under their wing, partly as a way of extending European influence inside the Ottoman Empire. Muslim resentment of this played a part in the massacres of Arab Christians in Lebanon and Syria in the 1860s.

In Palestine, according to the British census of 1918, there were about 700,000 Arabs and 56,000 Jews – that is, the Arabs formed about ninety percent of the population. Perhaps ten percent of the Arabs were Christians. Traditionally, relations seem to have been good among the different Palestinian communities. One unusual example of this, the way the three main groups would participate in one another's religious festivals, is still vividly recalled by many Palestinians today.

The Mount of Olives, one of the many ancient holy sites around Jerusalem that make Israel a place of such religious importance.

Zionism

By the early twentieth century a powerful new political movement was emerging that would change everything in Palestine. Zionism – which aimed to make the Jews an independent nation in the world, like other nations – was born in Eastern Europe in the late nineteenth century. At that time about five million Jews – almost two-thirds of the total world Jewish population – lived in Czarist Russia, where they were suffering increasing discrimination and persecution because of their different religious beliefs. Many were killed in anti-Jewish massacres – pogroms – that were encouraged or at any rate permitted by the authorities. The authorities also made it difficult for Jews to get jobs or enjoy a decent standard of living.

Anti-Semitism (anti-Jewish racism) became worse in the years leading up to the 1917 Russian Revolution, as the involvement of many Jews in the revolutionary underground made the government even more suspicious of the Jews as a whole. Pogroms and economic hardship forced about two and a half million Jews to leave Russia between 1881 and 1920, most settling in the United States or Western Europe.

The Zionist Commission arriving in Palestine, April 1918. The Commission was sent by European Jews to Palestine with the official mission of providing a link between the British authorities and the Jewish population. But the Zionists also hoped it would begin the task of establishing a Jewish state in Palestine.

Anti-Semitism was not confined to Eastern Europe. In 1894 Alfred Dreyfus, a French Jew, was falsely convicted in a French court of betraying his country and sentenced to life imprisonment. The case became an international scandal because of its exposure of anti-Semitism at the highest level in the West. One man profoundly influenced by the Dreyfus affair was Theodor Herzl, a Jew from Vienna who is today regarded as the founding father of Zionism. In a pamphlet published in 1896 Herzl said:

The nations in whose midst Jews live are all either covertly or openly anti-Semitic.

The only solution to the Jewish Question, he argued, was for the Jews to have a state of their own. As he put it:

Russian Jews being expelled from St. Petersburg, in the late nineteenth century. Anti-Jewish racism in Europe was the main reason for the emergence of Zionism as a political movement.

Let the sovereignty be granted us over a portion of the globe large enough to satisfy the rightful requirements of a nation; the rest we shall manage for ourselves.[2]

The next year, in August 1897, the first Zionist Congress was held in Basle, Switzerland. The first line of the program that the Zionist leaders adopted read:

The aim of Zionism is to create for the Jewish people a home in Palestine secured by public law.[3]

9

Why Palestine?

To understand why Zionists chose Palestine – then a predominantly Arab country, as we have seen – one has to go back almost to the very start of recorded history. The Bible tells how the Jews were led from Egypt to the Land promised them by God (the Exodus, an event historians trace to around 1300 BC), and how the Jewish kingdoms were established there. *Eretz Yisrael* – the land of Israel as Jews call it in Hebrew – was ruled continuously by the Jews for about 700 years until conquered by more powerful neighbors, who destroyed the Jewish Temple in Jerusalem and sent many Jews into exile. After the crushing of the Jewish Revolt in Palestine in AD 132, the Jewish presence there was reduced to a small, subject minority. After the exile and dispersal of the Jews elsewhere, the "Return to the Promised Land"

became an integral part of the Jewish faith, an idea that could also be interpreted spiritually, as a return to God's favor after being punished for sinning.

Modern Zionism, however, was conceived as a political, not a religious, movement. Its early leaders, inspired by both revolutionary socialism and European nationalism, were secular-minded men who considered hard before deciding on Palestine as the site for a future Jewish state. More religiously minded Jews, however, had already started settling in Palestine in small numbers

The Israelites march through the Wilderness – the flight of the Jews to the Promised Land, as told in the Bible, and here imagined by an eighteenth-century European artist.

Theodor Herzl, the founding father of Zionism. History would eventually prove his warning that European Jews were in terrible danger to be all too true, but during his lifetime few Jews supported his ideas.

by the turn of the century, and the idea of rebuilding *Eretz Yisrael* would clearly be a strong attraction of Zionism for Jews in general. What the early Zionist thinkers envisaged for the Arab population of Palestine is unclear. The slogan: "Land without a People for a People without a Land"[4] suggest some Jews were hardly aware of the existence of Palestinian Arabs. For others, the need to use force if the Arabs tried to resist their plans may have appealed to the Zionist philosophy of transforming Jews from passive subjects of the rule of others to active shapers of their own destinies. For some at least there is evidence they became disenchanted with Zionism when they realized what the implications were for the Arab inhabitants of Palestine.

Zionism at first attracted only a tiny percentage of Jews willing to put its political ideas into practice. This was perhaps not surprising. Besides the physical dangers and hardships of migrating to Palestine, Zionism challenged the Jews to re-define their own identity as a people. Despite anti-Semitism, many Jews had been assimilated into European society, and thought of themselves as English, French or whatever. There were also many Jews integrated into Arab society in the Middle East. In 1948 in Iraq, for example, there were 130,000 Jews who saw themselves first as Iraqis. As the Chief Rabbi of Iraq explained:

The Jews – and the Muslims – in Iraq just took it for granted that Judaism is a religion and Iraqi Jews are Iraqis.[5]

Britain's legacy

Lord Balfour (right) and Chaim Weizmann (left). Balfour's pledge of British support for Zionism changed the whole history of the Middle East.

In the Balfour Declaration of 1917 Britain promised to support the creation of a Jewish National Home in Palestine. One of the most important Zionist leaders at the time, Chaim Weizmann, called the Declaration "the golden key which unlocks the doors of Palestine." It is not difficult to see why Zionists thought the promise so important for their cause. Britain was still one of the most powerful countries on earth. It ruled Palestine. It would now help Jews to come and live there; its soldiers would protect them and help them to settle and develop the land. But why should the British government want to support such an idea?

There was some anti-Semitism in Britain too, and the arrival of many Jewish refugees escaping from persecution in Eastern Europe led to riots and demonstrations against them in the streets of London at the end of the nineteenth century. This affected to some extent the attitude of the British government toward the Zionists. The British prime minister at the time, David Lloyd George, once wrote:

> We have been trained even more in Hebrew history than in the history of our own country. I was brought up in a school where I was taught far more about the history of the Jews than about the history of my own land. I could tell you all the Kings of Israel. But I doubt whether I could have named half a dozen of the Kings of England, and not more of the Kings of Wales.[6]

Apart from political considerations, this tells you something about the emotional appeal of Zionism for at least some British politicians at the time.

The Balfour Declaration also promised to protect "the civil and religious rights of the existing non-Jewish communities," that is, the Arabs who then made up ninety percent of the population of Palestine. But if Palestine was to be the home of the world's Jews, what would happen to the Arabs? Lord Balfour's own views on the subject were revealed in a memorandum he wrote to the British cabinet in 1919:

The Four Great Powers are committed to Zionism. And Zionism, be it right or wrong, good or bad, is rooted in age-long traditions, in present needs, in future hopes, of far profounder import than the desires and prejudices of the 700,000 Arabs who now inhabit that ancient land.[7]

Looking back afterward, the conflict that developed between the Zionists and the Arabs of Palestine can be seen as the result of the various promises Britain made to both groups. The Arabs believed Britain had pledged itself to grant them independence, the Zionists that Britain had promised to help them establish a Jewish state – both in the same piece of land. There was no way both promises could be fulfilled at the same time. The writer Arthur Koestler commented after the State of Israel had been created in Palestine, that in the Balfour Declaration "one nation solemnly promised to a second nation the country of a third."

An anti-Jewish cartoon from an English magazine published in 1895, entitled "Presence of mind." It reveals much about "respectable" European society's opinion of Jews, and the extent to which such attitudes were publicly acceptable.

Drawing the frontiers of the Middle East

After World War I, two international conferences set the seal on the modern boundaries of the Middle East. At the Paris peace conference of 1919, Britain and France agreed to divide the area between them, basically as outlined by Sykes and Picot. The meeting in San Remo the following year of the League of Nations (the predecessor of today's United Nations) formally partitioned the Middle East into the French Mandates of Syria and Lebanon, and the British Mandates of Iraq and Palestine.

The Mandate system as such was designed to put checks on the administration of such subject territories by the colonial power, and to prepare their native peoples for eventual self-rule. The terms of the Palestine Mandate also made Britain responsible for putting the Balfour Declaration into effect. A completely new state, Transjordan (today, Jordan) was created at the same time along Palestine's eastern edge. Abdullah, the son of Hussein of Mecca, was installed by Britain as Transjordan's ruler – partly as a solution to an awkward area no one knew what to do with, partly as a consolation prize to the leaders of the Arab Revolt. With that, the battle-lines of the future Middle East conflict were all in place.

Not surprising was the reaction of the peoples of the region to having simply exchanged their Turkish overlords for European administrators, men who for the Arab Muslim majority were totally alien to their culture, religion and customs. The years that followed World War I could truly be called the Arab Awakening. The Arab Revolt had

At the end of World War I the League of Nations divided the Middle East into Mandates, to be administered by Britain and France.

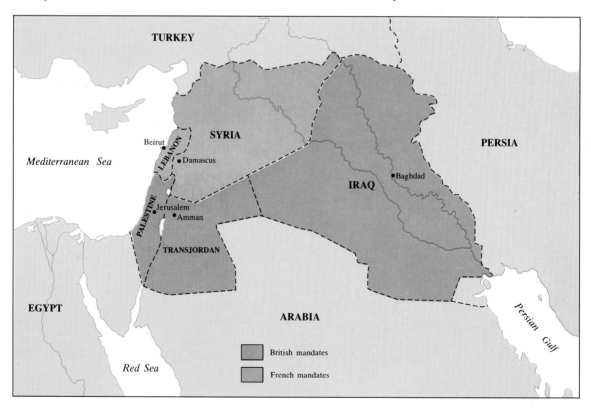

■	British mandates
■	French mandates

Religious friction between Jews and the mostly Muslim Palestinian Arabs often led to clashes. These disturbances in 1920 took place near the Dome of the Rock mosque in Jerusalem – an area that is holy to both Islam and Judaism.

failed to win the promised goal of independence, and had in any case been localized in its impact. Direct European rule of the Arab heartlands brought home the challenge posed by foreign domination, and it introduced modern political ideas – like nationalism and self-determination.

A class of Arab intellectuals now grew up determined to confront the challenge of the West. The Arab renaissance had two main centers: Egypt, where contact with the West began as early as 1798, when Napoleon Bonaparte invaded the country; and Syria and the Lebanon, where sizeable Christian communities had centuries-old links with Europe. Some of these intellectuals thought Islam was the natural banner around which to rally the masses, but it was the Christian-dominated movement inspired by the idea of Arab nationalism, with its emphasis on the unity of all the Arab peoples, that took precedence as a popular and effective force. The overriding aim of the nationalists was to end European rule, which they identified with subjugation and exploitation, and to assert Arab sovereignty and independence in all the Arab lands. The spread of such ideas throughout the region was in time helped by the advances in transportation and communications introduced by the West. The growing Arab nationalism also aroused ill feeling on the part of the Arabs of Palestine toward the Zionist settlers.

15

2
FOUNDATION OF A STATE
Between the wars 1918–39

THE PERIOD BETWEEN THE two World Wars, 1918–39, saw a massive increase in Jewish immigration into Palestine. The new waves of Zionist settlers were more politically minded, and more militant too. Many were inspired by Vladimir Jabotinsky, a Zionist leader who called for the use of force against the Arabs in order to establish a Jewish majority in Palestine. The Arab population became increasingly angry and frustrated as the European newcomers bought up all the land they could for farming. Eventually they began to build towns and cities on the land as well.

Violent clashes between the Arabs and Jews started to break out. In 1921 riots in Jaffa, the main port of entry for the immigrants, left 200 Jews and 120 Arabs dead or wounded. Jabotinsky set up a militia, the *Haganah* (Hebrew for "defense") to protect the Jewish settlements. In 1929, by which time there were more than 150,000 Jews in Palestine, there was widespread Arab–Jewish fighting. This was sparked off by a dispute at the main Jewish religious shrine of the Wailing Wall, in Jerusalem, which adjoins a Muslim holy site. The British authorities set up official inquiries into the causes of the violence, but, although some British officials were sympathetic to the Arabs' grievances, the government in London refused either to agree to their demands that Jewish immigration and land acquisition be halted or to grant them a representative voice in governing Palestine.

The confrontation came to a head in the 1930s, as the threat of Nazism in Germany made hundreds of thousands of Jews flee from Europe. One reason so many of these refugees went to Palestine was that other European countries and the United States refused to accept all but a handful. In 1936 the various Arab groups in Palestine united to form an Arab Higher Committee. In protest at the continued Jewish immigration, the Committee called a general strike, which developed into an all-out rebellion against both the Zionists and the British authorities. In 1937 another British commission of inquiry under Lord Peel declared that the terms of the Mandate were unworkable and recommended the partition of Palestine into separate Arab and Jewish states. The Arabs rejected this, and the rebellion was renewed even more fiercely. It took a concentrated

The British Lion in trouble in Palestine. It took Britain three years of sustained military effort to suppress the 1930s Arab rebellion in Palestine.

military effort by Britain, lasting a further eighteen months, to regain control in Palestine, by which time 101 British soldiers, 463 Jews and an estimated 5,000 Arabs had been killed. The core of the Palestine fighting force and leadership was destroyed.

With war looming in Europe, Britain could not afford so many troops tied up in Palestine, nor did it want to offend the other Arab countries and cause them to support Germany. After an abortive attempt to get representatives of the Palestinian Arabs and the Jews around a table in London, in May 1939 Britain issued a government policy statement in the form of a White Paper, which asserted that there was no intention that Palestine should become a Jewish state. Jewish immigration was limited, and was to be stopped altogether after five years. Britain promised to work for an independent state of Palestine within ten years. Now it was the Zionists' turn to feel betrayed.

▲ After World War II, Jewish survivors of the Nazi Holocaust flocked to Palestine – many of them arriving illegally, as on this overcrowded ship in 1947.

▼ British police break up an Arab demonstration in Jaffa, in 1933. Eventually, both Jews and Arabs saw the British troops in Palestine as their enemies.

The partition of Palestine

When the war ended in 1945 Britain found itself in a hopeless position over Palestine.

1 The world was deeply shocked to discover the full extent of the Nazi Holocaust against the Jews in Europe. Six million Jews – about one-third of the world's Jewish population – had been systematically murdered by the Nazis. Not only did this convince the Jews that the only hope for their future survival as a people lay in Zionism, it also won wide international support for the movement, especially from the rising new power in the world, the United States. Britain's efforts to enforce its promised immigration limits on the survivors of the Holocaust who flocked to Palestine were therefore deeply unpopular abroad.

2 Britain was exhausted materially and psychologically after five long years of war, and was heavily dependent on American aid.

3 Britain had to contend with attacks on its administration in Palestine from Jewish as well as Arab guerrillas. After the 1939 White Paper, Jabotinsky had come to the conclusion that the only way now to establish a Jewish state was "by the sword." In July 1946 a terrorist offshoot of the *Haganah* called the *Irgun*, led by Menachem Begin, carried out a bomb attack on the British headquarters

Eighty-eight people were killed in the explosion that destroyed the King David Hotel, Britain's administrative headquarters in Palestine in 1946.

18

in Palestine, the King David Hotel in Jerusalem. Eighty-eight people, Britons, Jews and Arabs, were killed, and British hopes of resolving the crisis, either politically or militarily, were ended.

After 1939, many Jews trying to enter Palestine in defiance of Britain's strict immigration quotas were rounded up to be imprisoned or deported.

In desperation, Britain appealed to the United Nations for help. On November 29, 1947, the UN General Assembly voted 33–13 to partition Palestine into Arab and Jewish states. Jerusalem, because of its special religious status for Jews, Muslims and Christians everywhere, was to be placed under international control. The UN Partition Plan allocated fifty-seven percent of the land, much of it thinly populated, to the Jews, who then formed about a third of the country's population. It was immediately rejected by the Palestinian Arabs, and Britain refused to try to implement it. Instead it announced it would give up the Mandate on May 15, 1948. In the civil war that

ensued, Arabs at first held the upper hand. The Zionist forces then went on the offensive. They took the ill-prepared Arabs by surprise, and 300,000 Palestinians fled their homes in fear of their lives. Whole Arab villages were destroyed, and many inhabitants were massacred by the *Irgun* and *Haganah*. One of the most notorious slaughters was at Deir Yassin where two-thirds of the inhabitants were brutally slaughtered and the rest were evicted. Amid the growing threat of all-out war between the Jews and the Arabs, the last British soldier left Palestine on May 14. Soon thereafter, the Jewish State of Israel was proclaimed.

Zionism and the Holocaust

Belsen concentration camp. When the Allies defeated Germany, the full extent of the Nazi program to exterminate Europe's Jews was revealed. "Never again" became a Zionist slogan.

Whatever the problems encountered by the Zionists in Palestine, the Nazi Holocaust proved that Zionism had been right about one thing – Jews had been in deadly danger in Europe. Most Jews had ignored the warnings given long before by Herzl and Weizmann, and the creation of Israel came too late to save them. The mass of European Jewry was now converted to Zionism. The memory of the Holocaust became a fundamental force in shaping Israel and its policies. A psychologist who carried out surveys of Israeli attitudes in the 1960s and 1970s wrote that:

> *The Jewish people regards itself as a nation of survivors, and no study of Israel, of Jewish identity and of the relationships between Jewish and other groups can ignore the profound implications of this background factor.*[8]

Many Israelis came to feel that the Arabs, and particularly the Palestinians, shared the violent hostility toward the Jews that the Nazis felt. They point out that during World War II the Palestinian leader Haj Amin al-Husseini sided with Hitler, who he hoped would help the Palestinians against Britain and the Zionists. The Holocaust has naturally most influenced Israel's European Jews (known in Hebrew as *Ashkenazim*). The growth in Israel's Oriental Jewish population (known in Hebrew as *Sephardim*), to the point where today they are a majority among the country's Jews, may reduce the importance of the Holocaust as a factor behind Israel's policies. But what has been called Israel's "siege mentality" seems likely to dominate the country for the foreseeable future. Menachem Begin, leader of the *Irgun* and later Israel's prime minister, used the pledge "Never again"[9] to justify many Israeli actions against the Arabs. The effect of such a slogan was calculated to unite a Jewish audience and stiffen its resolve.

The militant attitudes fostered by the Holocaust were not the only influences on the founders of Israel. Plans for the "rebirth of the Jewish nation" were highly idealistic. The best example of this is the *kibbutz* (Hebrew for a grouping, or gathering), originally a sort of agricultural settlement established in Palestine by the Zionist pioneers. A new form of communal living was developed in the *kibbutz*: all the members together own everything, and decisions are made democratically at general meetings. The socialist ideals of the *kibbutz* still exert a strong influence on Israeli society, although less than five percent of Israelis now live in this way. In fact, throughout most of Israel's history, egalitarianism has been the dominant political force in its domestic affairs.

▶ **Young people farming on an Israeli *kibbutz*, an institution dedicated to communal living, equality and democracy.**

◀ **Zionism: could the ends justify the means? This 1949 British cartoon questions not just the violent methods used by the Zionists in Palestine, but the whole direction of the movement.**

LONG AFFLICTED JEWISH PEOPLE

"SHORT CUT" TO **ZION** THROUGH A RIVER OF BLOOD

Arab bitterness

By the time the State of Israel was declared in the spring of 1948, the Palestinian Arabs had begun to develop a sense of national identity. A feeling that they were one distinct people had emerged as a result of their shared struggle against Britain and the Zionists. Similar nationalist feelings had grown up in the surrounding Arab countries, which were also engaged in fighting European occupation; but in Palestine the national awareness of the Arabs was sharpened by the additional challenge of Zionism. Some Zionists spoke of making Palestine as Jewish as England is English. Such statements made the Palestinians feel threatened for their culture, language and religion.

The Palestinians were mostly a peasant people, with a strong attachment to the land that they had farmed for countless generations. During 1948 over 700,000 Palestinians – over half the country's Arab population – fled their homes and farms, never to return. In Arabic, the Palestinians call this event simply *an-Nakbeh*, the Catastrophe. The lasting bitterness it has left lies at the heart of the Arab–Israeli dispute. The Palestinians believe the Zionists deliberately terrorized them into leaving in order to seize their land for the new Jewish state. One incident, the massacre on April 9, 1948 of

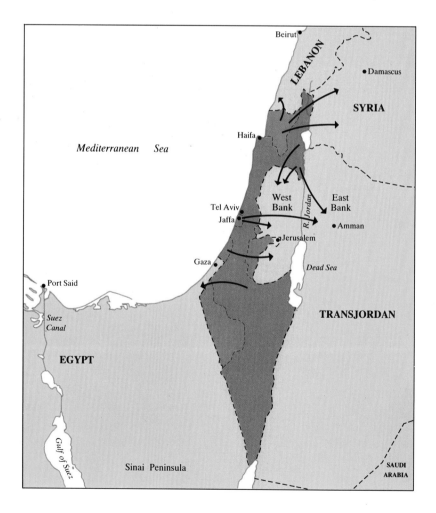

The blue area on the map is the area allocated to the Jews by the UN Partition Plan. The pink areas are those captured by Jews in 1948. More than half the Arabs of Palestine fled or were driven from their homes by the Zionists in 1948. The arrows indicate where the Arab refugees went.

◀Transjordanian armed forces on the move in May 1948. As the British Mandate in Palestine came to an end, Arab and Jew prepared for war.

▼The Palestinian Arabs had farmed the land of Palestine for years, as in this woodcut of the lower Himmon valley.

over 250 Arab civilians by the *Irgun* at the village of Deir Yassin, certainly helped trigger the mass flight of the Palestinians. There is now considerable evidence that there was a move by Jewish forces to oust Palestinians from various areas and to prevent them from returning.

Fawaz Turki is a Palestinian writer who grew up in one of the many refugee camps that sprang up around Israel to house the Arabs displaced in 1948. In his book *The Disinherited*, he describes how the Palestinian sense of identity was influenced by the experience of exile:

Our Palestinian consciousness, instead of dissipating, was enhanced and acquired a subtle nuance and a new dimension. It was buoyed by two concepts: the preservation of our memory of Palestine and our acquisition of education. We persisted in refusing the houses and monetary compensation offered by the UN to settle us in our host countries. We wanted nothing short of returning to our homeland. And from Syria, Lebanon and Jordan, we would see, a few miles, a few yards, across the border, a land where we had been born, where we had lived, and where we felt the earth. "This is my land," we would shout, or cry, or sing, or plead, or reason . . .[10]

Perhaps the Israelis should have foreseen what a powerful weapon of national identity they would be giving the Arabs who were driven out of Palestine. And given the prevailing climate of Arab nationalism, the rest of the Arab world reacted with predictable hostility to what happened to the Palestinians.

23

3
ISRAEL'S EARLY YEARS
The rise of Arab nationalism

THE FIRST REAL CHALLENGE to face the newly independent Arab states was the creation of Israel in their midst and the flood of Palestinian refugees into their territory. Their attempt to formulate a joint Arab military response was a dismal failure. Army units from Syria, Transjordan, Iraq and Egypt entered Palestine but were thrown back by the *Haganah*, whose fighters were not only better organized and equipped but were also filled with fervor in their desperate battle for Israel's survival. When armistice agreements were signed in 1949, Israel commanded eighty percent of Palestine.

The Arabs as a whole were outraged by what they felt was the injustice done to their fellow Arabs in Palestine, and they were angry at the humiliating defeat of their armies by Israel. Blame for the disaster fell on the Arab leadership, which still consisted mostly of regimes installed by Britain or France, and there was mounting unrest.

Within the next few years, King Abdullah of Jordan was assassinated as he went to pray in Jerusalem, a series of *coups d'état* shook Syria, serious riots broke out in Baghdad, and in Egypt a group of army officers seized power and exiled King Farouk. Radical Arab nationalism swept the region, directed both against "Western imperialism" and against Israel, which was regarded as another colonial occupier of Arab land. Jews living in the Arab countries were looked upon with increasing suspicion and hostility, and during the 1950s about half a million of them left to live in Israel.

The Arab leader who did more than anyone to spread and harness the tide of Arab nationalism was the head of the new military government in Egypt, Colonel Gamal Abdel Nasser. His fiery speeches calling for Arab unity and the "liberation of Palestine" were broadcast throughout the Middle East, and inspired a whole generation of Arabs.

Lieutenant-Colonel Gamal Abdel Nasser, soon after he took power in Egypt. The charismatic Nasser inspired the whole Arab world with his brand of Arab nationalism. But his promise to "liberate Palestine" was never fulfilled.

Britain and France – were they all washed up after their disastrous invasion of Egypt during the 1956 Suez Crisis? This political cartoon suggests that they were.

His defiance of the European powers, in particular Britain, led to the Suez Crisis of 1956.

When Nasser came to power in Cairo in 1954, Egypt had already obtained its independence from Britain, but a French-dominated company continued to run the Suez Canal. In July 1956 Nasser nationalized the Canal, giving Britain a reason to strike at the man it blamed most for its declining influence in the Middle East. Nasser's growing influence was also seen as a threat by Israel, and by France. It was thought he was encouraging the Arab rebellion in French-occupied Algeria. In October 1956 Israel invaded Egypt from the east as far as the Suez Canal, as part of a secret plan with Britain and France. A joint Anglo-French force then invaded Egypt from the north, under the pretext of separating the combatants and protecting the Canal for international shipping. The plot failed totally. The Egyptians rallied around Nasser, and Britain, France and Israel were forced to withdraw under pressure from the United States. Nasser was proclaimed a national hero by Arabs everywhere.

End of an era

U.S. President, Dwight D. Eisenhower. His determination forced Israel, Britain and France to withdraw from Egypt in 1956.

Looking back today, the Suez Crisis seems a minor episode compared with other wars before and after it. Out of the combined Anglo-French force of 22,000 troops sent to attack Egypt, 16 British and 10 French soldiers were killed. Some 200 Israelis, and as many as 3,000 Egyptians, many of them civilians, also lost their lives. Yet, despite the fact that no frontiers were redrawn, the Suez Crisis marked an important historical watershed. It exposed the inability of the European powers to control the independent nations of the Middle East any longer. The colonial age was over.

Almost overnight, Britain was replaced as the dominant outside power in the Middle East by the United States. The region was known by then to contain a large proportion (almost two-thirds) of the world's total oil reserves, and the strategic significance of the Middle East had long been clear to the Americans. The Middle East was geographically and politically important. This was the era of the Cold War between the superpowers, and the overriding American aim in the Middle East was to prevent Soviet influence from spreading there. This concern affected American attitudes toward the Middle East.

The United States emerged from the Suez Crisis as a neutral party. It had gained credit in Arab eyes for putting economic pressure on Britain and Israel to withdraw from Egypt. Israel had hoped for territorial gains from the war, but President Eisenhower was adamant that it must pull its troops out of every inch of the Sinai Peninsula and Gaza Strip that it had occupied.

Britain had tried to enlist American support in its campaign against Nasser by painting the Egyptian leader as a Soviet puppet in the region. In fact, although his brand of Arab nationalism was broadly socialist in principle, Nasser ruthlessly suppressed communist activists inside Egypt. However, despite his preference for a policy of non-alignment with either superpower, one powerful factor was pulling Nasser toward the Soviet camp. He wanted arms to counter what he saw as the growing threat to Egypt posed by Israel, but the Americans were reluctant to increase the supply of advanced weaponry to such an unstable area. Nasser signed his first arms deal with the Soviet satellite Czechoslovakia in September 1955, and the swift and decisive defeat of the Egyptian army by Israel in Sinai the following year only made him seek more Soviet military help. As Nasser developed his socialist policies, and became more involved with the USSR in the late 1950s and early 1960s, he was confirmed in the eyes of the United States as a dangerous enemy. With the encouragement of the influential Jewish community in the United States, Israel was built up as America's ally against the Soviet threat to the Middle East.

The polarization of the Arab–Israeli conflict along East–West lines quickly acquired a momentum of its own. The United States replaced France as Israel's main arms supplier, and the closer the U.S.–Israeli strategic alliance became, the more the Arab states confronting Israel turned to the USSR for help and protection. Soviet backing for the Arabs in turn justified and strengthened America's backing for Israel. This increased the possibility of confrontation in the Middle East between the superpowers.

The precarious situation in the Middle East has alarmed the West for decades. This cartoon appeared in 1956.

27

Birth of a nation

Israel has been called the superpower of the Middle East. Its series of crushing military victories over the combined armies of the Arab states gave it a power in the region out of all proportion either to the size of its territory or its population. How did it become so strong so quickly?

The Jewish population of Israel doubled in the first four years of its existence, and this created a host of problems through the need for rapid development of ways to support, unite and protect the population.

- The massive influx of immigrants had to be housed, fed and given work.
- People of many different cultures, languages and backgrounds had to be welded together into a single nation. Great energy and ingenuity was put into this task in Israel's early years.

- A massive development plan was undertaken in the lands left vacant by the Palestinians. Money poured in to finance this from Western governments and from wealthy Jewish communities abroad. New towns and settlements sprang up to replace the temporary camps for immigrants. Roads were built, power plants and cables installed, and a national water grid was devised that allowed previously desert areas to be irrigated and cultivated.
- All immigrants were taught Hebrew, the ancient language of the Jewish scriptures which the early Zionists had revived and modernized.
- Another unifying factor was military service, which all Jewish citizens, both men and women, were obliged to undergo at regular intervals throughout their active, adult life.

Jewish immigrants working in the fields in the 1950s. The new State of Israel undertook massive development plans to build a strong nation.

◄ The Israeli army has always called upon all Jewish citizens, women as well as men, to undergo weapons training. Army training helped to unify the immigrants into a nation.

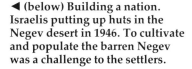

◄ (below) Building a nation. Israelis putting up huts in the Negev desert in 1946. To cultivate and populate the barren Negev was a challenge to the settlers.

The constant threat of war hanging over the Israelis also naturally encouraged national solidarity, and the biggest effort of all went into building a sophisticated, well-trained army, air force and navy. The success the Israelis achieved in creating the most powerful military force in the Middle East has to be judged in the light of the advantages they enjoyed over their Arab enemies. Israel was essentially founded by Europeans, who brought with them the education and expertise of the Western industrialized world. The *Haganah*, the forerunner of the Israel Defense Force (IDF), received its first assistance from British military experts. Then in the United States Israel found an ally that was prepared to supply and finance the most advanced weaponry available.

By contrast, the Arab states were Third World countries, starting from scratch. The frontline states that bore the brunt of the fighting had limited means and resources, on which their military programs were a heavy drain. And though on paper the combined Arab manpower and quantity of military equipment might seem impressive, in practice the Arab armies never operated effectively as a joint force. Political divisions among the Arab governments usually prevented coordinated planning or a truly unified military command.

4
GREATER ISRAEL
David and Goliath 1956–73

NASSER'S "TRIUMPH" OVER Britain and France at Suez raised high hopes among the Arab nationalists that a new era of Arab victories and glory had begun. However, despite the continued buildup of Soviet military equipment in Egypt and Syria, after several years there was still no sign of the great "liberation" of Palestine. In an attempt to defuse the growing sense of frustration, in 1964 the Arab states created the Palestine Liberation Organization (PLO). Meanwhile, a Palestinian named Yasser Arafat was setting up his own secret organization – *Fatah* – which was to be a purely Palestinian movement, independent of the Arab states. Through *Fatah* (meaning "victory" in Arabic), Arafat hoped to spur the Palestinians into action and, through attacks on Israel, to spark an all-out war.

Convinced that Israel was about to attack Syria, in May 1967 Nasser mobilized Egypt's forces in the Sinai. Israel's response was devastating. In a single day, June 5, 1967, Israel destroyed virtually the whole Egyptian air force on the ground in a surprise attack. In six days, it occupied the Gaza Strip and Sinai once more, while at the same time defeating Nasser's allies – Jordan to the east and Syria to the north. From Jordan it captured East Jerusalem and the West Bank, from Syria the important Golan Heights. Another 250,000 Palestinians were made refugees, most fleeing east into Jordan. All of Palestine was now in Israel's hands, plus

The repeated wars between Israel and the Arabs have made many regard peacekeeping in the Middle East as a hopeless task.

" OBSERVED ANY TRUCE YET?"

Egyptian soldiers crossing the Suez Canal toward Israeli-held territory in October 1973. The attack took the Israelis totally by surprise.

parts of Egypt and Syria, its two most powerful Arab enemies.

The Six-Day War of 1967 destroyed many of the dreams of the Arab nationalists, and for the Palestinians it killed the hope that the Arab states could regain their country for them by force. Instead they now flocked to join the guerrillas of *Fatah*. By 1970 the guerrillas were so powerful in Jordan (about half of whose population consisted of Palestinian refugees) that they threatened the government of King Hussein. Thus, in September of that year the king ordered the Jordanian army to attack the guerrillas (or *fedayeen*, which means "self-sacrificers" in Arabic). A bitter war followed in which at least 2,000 Palestinians were killed. The *fedayeen* were eventually crushed, and Jordan was thereafter denied them as a base from which to attack Israel.

President Nasser died in 1970 and was succeeded as President by Anwar Sadat. On October 6, 1973, having rebuilt the Egyptian army with the latest Soviet military technology, Sadat launched an attack across the Suez Canal into the Israeli-occupied Sinai. The 1973 war was not primarily about the Palestinian problem but was aimed at restoring the territory lost by Egypt and Syria in 1967. At the same time Syria attacked Israel from the north across the Golan Heights. Now it was the Israelis' turn to be taken by surprise, and the Arab armies cut deep into Israel's defenses. The Israelis mobilized their forces for a counterattack, and launched one that was so successful, in fact, that there was a risk of direct Soviet intervention in defense of Moscow's Arab allies. Negotiations between the Americans and the Soviets led to a ceasefire on October 23 – after Washington had placed U.S. nuclear forces on a worldwide alert.

The myth of invincibility

Not long before the 1973 war, General Ariel Sharon, then an army commander but later to become Israel's defense minister, boasted that:

> *Israel is now a military superpower . . . All the forces of the European countries are weaker than we are . . . Israel can in one week conquer the area from Khartoum to Baghdad and Algeria.*[11]

Such confidence in Israel's military superiority over the Arabs was not entirely unjustified. The country's armed forces had become much more powerful than they were in 1967, when they had defeated the combined Arab armies in just six days. On the map below you can find Israel's post-1967 borders with Egypt, Jordan and Syria. It is not hard to see what natural advantages the Suez Canal and the Sinai desert, the Jordan River and the Golan Heights gave

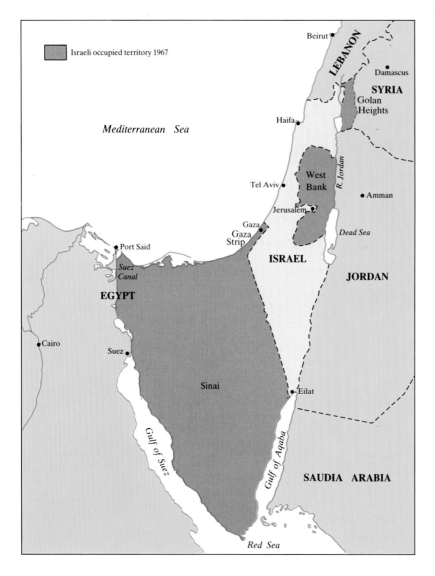

Israeli occupied territory 1967

In the Six-Day War of 1967, Israel captured the last remaining areas of Mandate Palestine – the West Bank and Gaza Strip – as well as the Egyptian Sinai Peninsula and the Syrian Golan Heights. The Sinai was later returned to Egypt.

Israel for its defense. Israel was the only country in the Middle East with the technological base to develop its own advanced weapons. (Between 1967 and 1971 Israel's scientific output was double that of the whole Arab world.) And with financial and military support from the United States, it was not surprising that on the eve of the 1973 war the Israelis felt they had little to fear.

This false sense of security was partly responsible for the way Egypt and Syria were able to take the Israelis so totally by surprise. The advantage of surprise attack was not the only lesson the Arabs had learned from 1967. Evident in the performance of Arab forces were innovation (the Egyptians used high-powered water hoses to blast a way across the banks of the Suez Canal and so through Israel's "impregnable" Bar Lev defense line), better organization, and better equipment. Soviet-supplied antiaircraft missiles, for instance, were effectively used to offset Israel's greatest military advantage – its powerful air force. In the war 2,800 Israelis were killed and 8,000 wounded; 840 of Israel's tanks and 120 planes were destroyed. Arab losses were far higher: over 20,000 killed, and over 60,000 wounded. Seen in proportion to its small population, however, Israel's losses were equivalent to more than twice those suffered, for example, by the United States in the whole ten years of its involvement in the Vietnam War. The 1973 war overturned all the conventional thinking about the Arab–Israeli balance of power. This is how an Israeli military correspondent described the effect at the time:

> In less than twenty-four hours, Israel was transformed from a military power, even in global concepts, from a state with an army the fame of which had become a model to the world; from a country which – six short years ago – had won the most brilliant victory in the history of modern warfare; from a state which, according to her leaders' declarations, had "an army that was never in a better state" – to a country fighting with clenched teeth for its very existence. A country living under the shadow of extermination.[12]

Before the war, the Israeli soldier had seemed something of a superman, invincible. Now on Arab television, Israeli prisoners of war were paraded for the first time.

The Palestine "revolution"

Yasser Arafat, chairman of the Palestine Liberation Organization, is the only leader most Palestinians will acknowledge – but he is an untrustworthy terrorist in the eyes of Israel.

By 1970, the strength of the Palestinian guerrilla force, *Fatah,* and its popularity throughout the Arab world, were so great that the group was able to take over the PLO and elect Yasser Arafat as its leader. From this time on, the Arab governments were forced to accept the presence among them of an independent PLO, but it was often a highly uncomfortable relationship. On the Palestinian side, there was deep resentment at the failure of the Arab regimes to match their rhetoric in support of the Palestinian cause with effective action to regain what had been lost to Israel.

The armed Palestinian groups that sprang up in the late 1960s and early 1970s (of which *Fatah* was only the first, although it remained the largest) were determined to rely on their own efforts in the future, and to mobilize all Palestinians, wherever they were, in the struggle against Israel. This is what Palestinians mean by their "revolution" – a term some of them interpreted more widely than others. For Yasser Arafat's *Fatah,* regaining the Palestinian homeland took precedence over everything else. For other Palestinian factions, like the heavily

Marxist-influenced Popular Front for the Liberation of Palestine (PFLP) and Democratic Front for the Liberation of Palestine (DFLP), the "revolution" was directed as much against the Arab governments as against Israel.

Whatever the Arab governments really thought about the PLO, outwardly they had no choice but to support it, because it represented the Palestinian cause, and hence the focus of Arab nationalism. The main contenders for leadership of the Arab world, Egypt, Syria and Iraq, competed with one another to win the PLO's loyalty and so to be known as the champions of the Arab cause. Some countries sponsored their own PLO factions. Any Arab country that allowed the PLO to maintain a presence on its territory, however, took a major risk: that of Israeli retaliation. Every *fedayeen* incursion into Israel was swiftly followed by reprisal raids – first, against Egypt under Nasser, then Jordan in the 1960s, and finally against Lebanon in the 1970s and 1980s. These raids often inflicted heavy casualties and damage and were designed to turn the Arab countries against the PLO.

After Israel occupied the West Bank and Gaza Strip in 1967, many in the PLO, inspired by the guerrilla warfare against the Americans in Vietnam, thought of waging a "popular war of liberation" against the occupation forces, but Israel quickly crushed the armed Palestinian resistance to its rule, and sealed its borders against attack or infiltration from outside. Militarily, the PLO remained an almost insignificant threat to Israel. Its efforts to take over the functions of a government for the displaced Palestinians were far more successful, however Lebanon, which became the or̴ tion's base after its expulsion from the PLO set up schools, factories and other facilities for the n̴ a million Palestinian refugees living ther̴

▶ A Palestinian refugee camp in Damascus, Syria – just one of many that surround Israel's borders. The camps are a breeding ground for the despair and frustration that feed Palestinian violence.

◀ Teaching programs for refugee children, run by the special United Nations organization UNRWA, have helped make the Palestinians today the best-educated community in the Arab world.

Territory for peace?

Israel after the Six-Day War of June 1967 was a very different country from the one that preceded it. When the state was founded in 1948, some 165,000 Palestinians – the minority who did not flee their homes – came under its control. These Palestinians were eventually incorporated into the state with citizenship rights (today they and their descendants form almost one-fifth of Israel's population). In 1967, however, the conquest of the territories of the West Bank and Gaza (known as the occupied territories) brought nearly a million more Palestinians under Israeli rule.

The question of what Israel should do with the occupied territories was not a simple one. Should they be returned to the Arabs in return for a peace treaty? Or kept as bargaining chips for the future? Comparing the shape of Israel including and excluding

Protest with slogans rather than stones. These Arabs are integrated into Israel, but they tend to have the worst jobs, and they say they are discriminated against.

the occupied territories on the map on page 32, you can see why many Israelis believed their country could be adequately defended only by holding on to the West Bank. Before 1967 Israel's waist was so narrow that an invading army might easily cut the country in half. However, if Israel kept the occupied territories, what would happen to their large Arab population? Annexing them outright, and making their inhabitants citizens with the right to vote in elections, would bring about a dangerous shift in the balance between Jews and Arabs inside the state. Because of the Arabs' higher birthrate, annexation would risk the Jews' being outnumbered by the Arabs in time. This threat has been called Israel's demographic time-bomb. Israelis who oppose the annexation of the occupied territories argue that a Greater Israel (that is, one expanded to include the West Bank and Gaza Strip) cannot be both Jewish and democratic.

In the end, Israel did not change the legal status of the occupied territories to make them part of Israel, with the exception of Arab East Jerusalem. This Israel annexed and declared part of its "eternal, undivided capital," although the city was not recognized internationally as such. The army continued to run the occupied territories, and its Palestinian inhabitants, who today number about one and a half million, were not given the vote or other civil rights. What Israel did do, however, was change the physical status of these areas, by building towns, settlements and roads that linked them to Israel proper. Today some 70,000 Jewish settlers live in the occupied West Bank (which Israel calls by its Biblical names of Judea and Samaria) and Gaza Strip. Many Israelis regard these areas simply as part of their country, and Israeli maps no longer show any border between them and pre-1967 Israel. Nevertheless, if the Palestinians are ever to have a homeland, most opinion outside Israel seems to agree it can only be the West Bank and Gaza. Depending on the point of view, there are strong arguments both for and against this proposal.

The Dome of the Rock mosque in Jerusalem. Muslims worldwide deeply resent the Israelis' occupation of this, the third holiest site in Islam.

5
A PEACE OF SORTS
Camp David Treaty

IT REQUIRED THE COOPERATION of both superpowers to end the 1973 Arab–Israeli war, but from as early as July 1972, when Egypt ended its close alliance with Moscow by expelling all Soviet military advisers, it was clear that President Sadat was moving toward the United States. In 1977 there was a joint U.S.–Soviet Declaration on Middle East peace. Then, on November 19 of that year, Sadat amazed the whole world when he flew to Jerusalem to make a speech to Israel's parliament, the Knesset, calling for peace.

For the other Arab states confronting Israel, Sadat's dramatic peace gesture went against the fundamental principles of Arab unity. In Arab eyes, Egypt was abandoning the Palestinian cause in return for American financial and other help. In September 1978, Sadat and Israeli Prime Minister Begin accepted U.S. President Carter's invitation to hold talks at the presidential retreat of Camp David, Maryland, out of which came two agreements. One provided for the return to Egypt of the Israeli-occupied Sinai. The second, entitled "A Framework for Peace," was intended to solve the Palestinian problem – Sadat hoped this would satisfy his Arab critics that he was not betraying the Palestinians by entering into a separate peace with Israel.

On March 26, 1979, a treaty was signed in Washington formally ending thirty-one years of war between Egypt and Israel. According to "A Framework for Peace," Jordan and the Palestinians were supposed to join Egypt in talks with Israel about Palestinian autonomy in the occupied West Bank and Gaza Strip, but Jordan and the Palestinians, along with virtually the entire Arab world, rejected the whole process that

► Israel's invasion of Lebanon in June 1982. Nine armored divisions, 90,000 troops and one of the world's most powerful air forces were sent to attack PLO guerrilla forces of less than 10,000. Against all odds, the PLO held out in encircled Beirut for almost two months before agreeing to leave Lebanon.

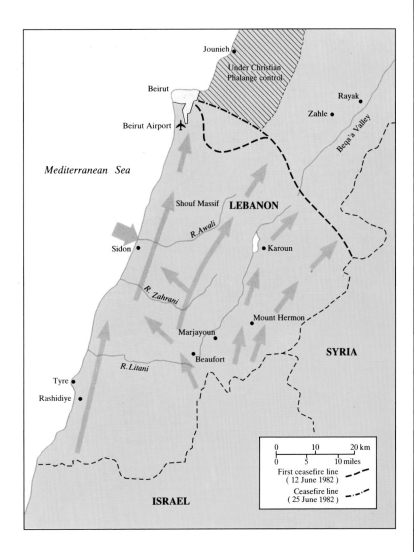

◄ (facing page) President Sadat of Egypt (left), President Carter of the United States (center) and Prime Minister Begin of Israel (right) celebrate the signing of the Camp David Peace Treaty in Washington in March 1979.

had begun at Camp David. In retaliation for the peace treaty, the Arab states imposed a total economic and political boycott of Egypt, whose membership in the Arab League was suspended.

With its Egyptian flank secure, Israel was freer to engage the other Arab states more actively. In March 1978 Israel attacked southern Lebanon in an operation against Palestinian guerrilla bases there. In June 1981 the Israeli air force bombed and destroyed an Iraqi nuclear installation, and in December 1981 Israel announced that it had annexed the Syrian Golan Heights. In June 1982, Begin's right-wing government

launched its most ambitious military plan of all: a full-scale attack aimed at the final destruction of the PLO. After the Israelis had besieged the PLO's headquarters in the Lebanese capital Beirut for two months, killing many thousands of civilians, the Palestinian guerrillas agreed to leave the country. Soon after their evacuation, Christian Lebanese gunmen loyal to Israel carried out a large-scale massacre of Palestinian refugees in the Beirut camps of Sabra and Chatila. Many Israelis were deeply opposed to the whole Lebanese venture, and it left the most serious internal divisions in Israel's history.

The cold peace

President Anwar Sadat of Egypt. The West praised him for making peace with Israel, but the other Arabs denounced him as a traitor. He was assassinated in 1981.

Whatever the successes and failures of the Camp David Treaty, a decade later it cannot be denied that it has stood the test of time. But what has it achieved beyond ending the state of war between Israel and Egypt? The answer depends on the different expectations of the parties involved, as outlined in the points below.

1 Israelis have been disappointed at the cold formality of relations with Egypt, and the lack of contact in trade and tourism.
2 Egyptians had hoped for increased economic prosperity as a result of large-scale U.S. aid, and the freeing of funds from the war effort, but this has failed to materialize for the vast majority of people. Opponents of the government's alliance with the United States focus their anger and resentment on the Camp David Treaty.
3 Most Israelis would probably agree that the benefits of Camp David have outweighed its costs. Giving up the barren Sinai was regarded as a price worth paying for neutralizing Egypt and dividing the anti-Israel Arab front.

4 Egypt's isolation in the Arab world proved to be only a temporary penalty for making peace with Israel. Under the threat posed by non-Arab Iran in the Gulf War, most of the Arab states, led by Iraq, have gradually restored their ties with Egypt. If worse came to worse, the Arab governments felt, only Egypt's military strength could stem the tide of Iran's Islamic revolutionaries.

Those who perhaps really paid the price for Camp David were President Sadat – assassinated in October 1981 – and the Syrians, Lebanese and of course Palestinians who subsequently bore the brunt of the 1982 Israeli attack. For the Palestinians, the Camp David Treaty was the worst of what they see as the many betrayals of their cause by the Arab states. The new Arab–Israeli balance of power after 1973 raised hopes among the Palestinians that Israel would agree to withdraw from the occupied territories in return for a peace treaty. These hopes were then boosted by two developments: Arab recognition of the PLO and its claim to the occupied territories, and a superpower agreement on the Middle East in 1977. Nearly all Arabs believe that, because of the close alliance between Israel and the United States, the Americans are not neutral enough to mediate in the conflict, and that Soviet involvement in the peace process is also needed to obtain the minimum the Arabs will accept in a settlement.

Among Israelis there have always been fears that the Camp David Treaty may not survive the future, and that Egypt's powerful armed forces will be thrown back into the anti-Israeli Arab military alliance. What would happen, they wondered, if the government in Egypt were to be overturned? Having survived the assassination of Sadat in 1981, and Israel's invasion of Lebanon in 1982, the durability of the treaty now seems more assured in Israeli eyes, especially as Sadat's successor, President Hosni Mubarak, has managed to re-integrate Egypt into the Arab world without compromising his country's commitment to peace with Israel.

Peace with Israel brought few of the promised benefits for Egypt's teeming millions, despite a massive American aid program. The grinding poverty many Egyptians still suffer threatens the country's future stability.

The war of words

The strength of Western support for Israel has led many Arabs to believe that at the heart of their conflict with the Jewish state lies a struggle against the United States and its allies in the Western world. Despite Arab efforts to promote their side of the conflict in the West, for most of the history of the conflict the Arabs have failed. Given such factors as European feelings of guilt over the Holocaust, and the presence of influential Jewish communities in most Western countries, this is perhaps not surprising. However, in the rest of the Muslim and Third World countries, and in the Communist bloc, the Arabs have been almost universally successful in winning support for their cause.

The way the world as a whole is divided between support for Israel and support for the Palestinians is clearly reflected in the efforts of the United Nations, which has grappled for most of its existence with the problem of finding a solution to the conflict.

The UN General Assembly (in which all member states are represented) "voted Israel into existence" in 1947. However, since that time resolutions supporting Palestinian national rights and condemning Israel's behavior toward the Arabs have commanded overwhelming majorities. In 1975 the General Assembly passed a resolution claiming that the regime in occupied Palestine was racist in structure, and denouncing Zionism as a "form of racism and racial discrimination."

In the UN Security Council, the United States, along with the four other permanent members (the USSR, China, Britain and France) has the power to veto any resolution submitted. It has regularly used this veto to defend Israel. After the Six-Day War of 1967,

A UN Emergency Force was sent to Suez in 1956, to act as a buffer between the two sides. This cartoon suggests that they were ineffective.

"ER — ARE YOU GUARDING ME — OR AM I GUARDING YOU ?"

the Security Council did, however, agree on Resolution 242, setting out the basis for a peace settlement – a resolution that was endorsed by Israel and all the Arab states. Like everything else in the war of words over the Palestine issue, Resolution 242 has been the subject of endless debate and sharply differing interpretations. Its main recommendations, however, are clear enough: Israeli withdrawal from the occupied territories and Arab acceptance of Israel's "right to live in peace within secure and recognized boundaries."

For many years the PLO would not explicitly accept Resolution 242. In Israeli eyes, this was because the PLO is a terrorist organization dedicated to the destruction of Israel. According to the Palestinians, their objection was that 242 refers to the Palestinians only as refugees, and makes no mention, as other UN resolutions do, of the Palestinians' right to self-determination – that is, to independent statehood if they wish. The result of this was deadlock, with

The UN General Assembly. Many member states are critical of Israel's treatment of the Palestinians – but U.S. support has shielded Israel from international sanctions.

Israel unwilling to talk to the PLO, and the PLO unwilling to surrender its last card of giving recognition to Israel without a guarantee of receiving something tangible for the Palestinians in return. However, on November 15, 1988, at a session of the Palestine National Council (PNC) in Algiers, the equivalent of the Palestinian parliament, Yasser Arafat attempted to break the stalemate by declaring the existence of a Palestinian state in the occupied territories. He also accepted UN Resolution 242, which effectively meant recognizing the State of Israel. It was a blow for moderation from the Palestinians which put pressure on Israel. The question now was whether an international peace conference would be able to persuade both sides to compromise and cooperate sufficiently to achieve a negotiated solution to the Arab–Israeli issue.

The new Israel

Israel today is a very different country from that dreamed of by the early Zionist pioneers. Since the state's creation, a new generation has grown up, for whom war with the Arabs is a permanent fact of life. The socialist principles pursued by Israel's first leaders have been increasingly replaced by another type of Zionism that stresses conquest of the land and an aggressive, uncompromising attitude toward the Arabs. In 1977 the right-wing Likud Party led by Menachem Begin was voted into power in Israel. The Labor Party has not won an outright majority in any general election since.

Shimon Peres, leader of Israel's Labor Party since 1977. He was prime minister from 1984 to 1986 and has held a number of positions in other coalition governments.

More than any other factor, the change in Israel's character can be traced to the 1967 war and the acquisition of power over a large population of Palestinians. Israel's military occupation of the West Bank and Gaza Strip has been criticized by many, not least by the Israelis themselves. In the words of Professor Yeshayahu Leibowitz, of the Hebrew University in Jerusalem, the occupation has "transformed Israel into a conquering power, an instrument for the violent domination of another people . . . The occupation has corroded Israel's social fabric and led to a belief in the utility of force to solve political problems."[13]

Harsh methods have been used to crush Palestinian resistance to Israeli rule. This is how Dr. Albert Aghazarian, a lecturer at the Palestinian University of Bir Zeit in the West Bank, described life under Israeli occupation in 1986:

> *Two hundred thousand Palestinians have been imprisoned since 1967. That is one out of six of the population . . . You have forty-eight percent of the land taken, you have ten thousand houses demolished . . . You have over one thousand two hundred leaders of the community who have been deported . . .*[14]

Israel's treatment of the Palestinians of the West Bank and Gaza Strip, many of whom work inside Israel in menial, poorly paid jobs, has been compared with South Africa's treatment of its black population.

A central element of the Likud Party's policy has been to ensure that the occupied lands be added permanently to Israel's territory. For this purpose Jewish settlement was greatly encouraged in these areas. When Menachen Begin came to power in 1977 there were 5,000 settlers in 36 outposts in the occupied territories. Today there are some 120 settlements, with a population of around 70,000.

Disputes between the settlers, and the Palestinians over land rights and scarce water resources are frequent, as are violent clashes. The Israeli religious settler group Gush Emunim has taken the lead in establishing Jewish outposts in the occupied territories. This is how one Gush Emunim settler explained why she went to live in the West Bank:

> *Jewish people come here not because of political reasons, not because of security reasons, but because this land was promised to them by the Lord.*[15]

◄ When Israel returned the Sinai Peninsula to Egypt in 1982, the new border cut some communities in half. Here a Palestinian tries to communicate with those on the other side in Egypt, across what has become known as the shouting fence.

► Israeli soldiers on patrol in Arab East Jerusalem. These soldiers are members of Israel's Arabic-speaking Druze community, and are often used by Israel to police Palestinian trouble spots.

6
FORTY YEARS LATER
The Middle East today

THE ARAB WORLD TODAY is full of contra-dictions and extremes: there is enormous wealth in the oil-rich states and oppressive poverty elsewhere; there are both absolute monarchies and Marxist republics; barren deserts and rich farmland; the latest modern technology and social conditions that have changed little since medieval times. The potential of the area as a whole in both natural and human resources is immense, as shown by the rapid development that has taken place over a relatively short period, but this development has brought its own problems and challenges.

The Arab economic boom set off by the sharp rise in the price of oil after the 1973 war, and again after the Iranian revolution

Twenty years of life under Israeli occupation erupted into open Palestinian rebellion in December 1987. Despite the deaths of some 400 Palestinians, the uprising – or *Intifada* in Arabic – shows no sign of subsiding.

of 1979, carried with it the seeds of its own destruction, because it forced the oil-consuming countries to make energy cut-backs and find alternative sources of fuel. The consequent oil surplus and declining prices brought hardship to many of the poorer Arab countries that benefited indi-rectly from oil revenue. The problems of economic decline are made worse by high population growth. From 1970, at the pres-ent rate, the population of the Arab coun-tries will almost double by the year 2000.

Poverty, inflation, unemployment and social and political tensions provide fertile ground for the rising political force in the region, Muslim fundamentalism.

Similar challenges face the Palestinians of the occupied territories: rapid population growth, with three-quarters of the population under the age of twenty-one; expectations and political awareness raised by universal education, but limited economic or employment opportunities. Continued military occupation and Jewish settlement over twenty years have steadily increased Palestinian resentment of Israel's rule over the West Bank and Gaza. In December 1987 the anger and frustration of Palestinians in the occupied territories erupted into a popular uprising lasting over a year.

Israel has been insulated from many of the problems affecting the Arab world. What it has shared with its neighbors is a state of constant war or threat of war that has diverted a large part of its national resources into military expenditure. Tensions among Jews have become more serious: between the religious and secular-minded, between Oriental and European Jews, between left and right. Since the 1982 Lebanese war, political polarization has advanced steadily, making consensus in government harder to achieve. A coalition of the left and right has been in power in Israel since 1984, but the Labor and the Likud parties have been unable to agree on the future of the occupied territories and peace with the Arabs. In addition to the country's economic and political problems is the threat of declining immigration and growing emigration. In 1988 over ninety percent of Jews allowed to leave the USSR chose to settle elsewhere than in Israel.

The next generation of Palestinians. What will the future hold for these children in Jerusalem? Continued occupation, a state of their own, or more violence?

The mosque and the synagogue

Religion has always been a potentially explosive factor in the Arab–Israeli conflict. Today, even with the growth of religious militancy among both Muslims and Jews, the great majority of Israelis still see the conflict as being in essence about their country's security, while most Palestinians would view it as a struggle for political rights. Nevertheless, the minority of religious extremists on both sides is an increasingly important factor.

The geographical focus of the Arab–Israeli conflict is also the religious focus of the three great world faiths: Judaism, Islam and Christianity. Nowhere is the religious dimension of the conflict more apparent than in Jerusalem, a Holy City for Christians, Jews and Muslims. There is a history of

Orthodox Jews and soldiers worship together at the Western Wall. Some Orthodox Jews are staunchly anti-Zionist and do not recognize the State of Israel.

violent clashes between Jews and Muslims over the city's religious shrines. The Jewish Wailing Wall, a remnant of the ancient Jewish Temple, also forms part of the base of the Muslim Noble Sanctuary, which contains the al-Aqsa and Dome of the Rock mosques. Muslims believe the Prophet Muhammad ascended to heaven from here. The perceived threat posed by Israel to the Islamic sites of Jerusalem is an important factor in the hostility felt toward the Jewish state by the Muslim world as a whole.

There is a historic and theological basis to the hostility between Islam and Judaism, but the scriptures of both religions can also be (and are) used to call for tolerance and peaceful coexistence between the two. Such voices attract far less attention, however, than those of the religious extremists. In Israel, Rabbi Meir Kahane, whose Kach Party won a seat in Israel's parliament in the 1984 election, has come to represent the

Jerusalem, the holy city of the world's three main religions – Islam, Christianity and Judaism – remains at the very heart of the Arab–Israeli conflict.

growing support, especially among the young, of religiously motivated anti-Arab views. The following is typical of Kahane's appeals to his fellow Israelis:

> *It's time to realize we didn't come here to create a Western democracy. We wanted to end our troubles, be a majority in our own land. When I run Israel, Jews will always be the majority. Because we won't have Arab citizens.*[16]

Kahane and his Kach party were banned from running for office in Israel's 1988 election on the grounds that they advocated racism. By then, however, Kahane's demand that the Palestinians be forcibly expelled from Israel and the occupied territories had gained some acceptance in right-wing Israeli circles.

The "Death to Israel" slogan of the Islamic Revolution in Iran in 1977 revealed the extent to which hostility toward the Jewish state has become a religious issue among many Muslims. "Death to U.S. Imperialism" is another slogan of the Iranian Revolution, which is violently opposed to all Western influence in the region, whether political, cultural, economic or military. The close ties between Israel and the United States reinforce this dual hostility, which has found support among mainstream Sunni Muslims of the Arab world, including the Palestinians.

Politics and religion clearly make for a dangerously explosive mixture in the Middle East. It is an interesting question whether the destabilizing effects of religious militancy are a cause or a product of the Arab–Israeli conflict.

What price peace?

The Arab–Israeli conflict has lasted more than forty years, taking the creation of Israel as the starting point. Throughout the conflict, proposals for a settlement have been put forward from every quarter, and the failure of all these attempts to find a solution stems not just from the depth of hostility involved, great though that is, but also from the fact that so many conflicting outside interests, up to superpower level, have become entangled in the situation.

The main hope for progress in the Middle East peace process today is to hold an international conference presided over by the

A Boeing 707 that was hijacked by Arab terrorists on August 30, 1969 sits shattered by a bomb on the runway at Damascus.

superpowers and the other permanent members of the UN Security Council. Originally a Soviet proposal, it has since gained support from all the Arab states, including the PLO, from the countries of the European Economic Community (EEC), and, with qualifications, from the United States. Israel itself is divided over the conference proposal, with the Labor Party supporting it and the Likud rejecting it.

It is hard to tell what sort of settlement might be agreed upon between the Palestinians and the Israelis even if they could be brought face to face in such a forum. Among nearly all the parties there is a broad consensus now about exchanging territory for peace, the principle first agreed in the UN's Resolution 242. But no Israeli government, now or in the foreseeable future, is likely to agree to the PLO's demand for an independent Palestinian state in all of the occupied territories, with East Jerusalem as its capital. The most the mainstream left wing in Israel is prepared to discuss is the so-called Jordanian option. This envisages an agreement with the government of Jordan, in which non-PLO Palestinians might participate, whereby the non-strategic parts of the West Bank, excluding Jerusalem, would be returned to some form of Jordanian control.

There are important internal divisions within each of the Israeli and Palestinian camps. The PLO has a "rejectionist" wing, backed by radical Arab states like Syria and Libya, which vows to continue the armed struggle until all of Palestine is liberated. In Israel the Likud vows never to give up an inch of *Eretz Yisrael*. At the other end of the spectrum, and still very much in the minority, there are combined Arab–Jewish peace groups inside Israel, and left-wing Israelis who regularly defy the law in Israel by traveling abroad to meet with moderate PLO members. Optimists in the peace camp have sometimes argued that the similarity between the Palestinian and Jewish experiences ought to make for a natural bond of understanding between the two peoples. They point out that the Palestinians, too, are an oppressed people now scattered all over the world who long to return to their land and build their own nation. Some have even called the Palestinians the "new Jews."

A member of Israel's "Peace Now" movement confronts an Israeli soldier in the occupied West Bank. "Peace Now" gained a lot of support after the 1982 invasion of Lebanon.

What price war?

◄ In Jordan, children as young as eight years old are taught to use machine guns. Future generations are already involved in the conflict.

▼ President Hafez al-Assad of Syria – Israel's most dangerous enemy today in the Arab world. Syria's acquisition of long-range missiles and chemical weapons causes Israel increasing concern.

To most outsiders, a so-called military solution to the conflict in the Middle East has long since ceased to exist. The PLO's continued adherence to the doctrine of armed struggle seems senseless when in over twenty years it has not regained a single inch of Palestine, nor could it ever hope to match the armed forces of Israel. On the other hand, Israel cannot destroy the PLO, which, as the Palestinians point out, is in essence an idea that cannot be defeated through warfare. But this logic is of little use against an Israel that argues that it must either maintain its military superiority or face annihilation, or against Arabs who say that fewer than 5 million Israelis cannot dominate 160 million Arabs indefinitely.

Today's President Hafez al-Assad of Syria sees himself as the new Saladin, the hero of Arab history who recaptured Jerusalem from the Crusaders in 1187. His masterful manipulation of the Middle East chessboard, and his determination to make Syria the equal of Israel in strength, have made Syria a foe to be reckoned with. Since the 1973 war, the Israeli–Syrian confrontation has mostly been carried on indirectly in

A military parade in the Egyptian capital, Cairo. Egypt has been at peace with Israel for over a decade. But can the peace survive the future?

Lebanon. The threat that this could one day turn into a direct Israeli–Syrian war is always present, and because of the close military alliances between Syria and the USSR, and between Israel and the United States, this in turn raises the threat of a superpower confrontation.

The arms race in the Middle East has itself already acquired the potential for a conflagration of horrific proportions even without outside intervention. Although Israel refuses to confirm or deny persistent reports that it has developed its own nuclear bomb, there is no longer any doubt that it has long possessed a nuclear weapons capability. A number of Arab states also have access to nuclear technology, although none is yet thought to have developed a bomb. It was the belief that Iraq was on the threshold of producing its own nuclear weapons that led Israel to destroy Iraq's nuclear plant outside Baghdad in 1981.

The balance of conventional military forces in the Middle East is also changing fast. There has been an increase in numbers of long-range missiles in the region. Iraq, Syria and Libya have been supplied with Soviet surface-to-surface missiles, while Saudi Arabia has bought and deployed Chinese missiles. Israel has tested its own long-range missile, and Egypt is believed to be in the process of developing one.[17] The Gulf War showed the effectiveness of another weapon: poisonous chemical gases. Chemical weapons are believed to have been developed by Syria, Israel and Egypt as well as Iraq, Iran and Libya. Biological warfare is yet another menace. The threat of long-range missiles being used to launch chemical warheads is one that Israel takes very seriously today.

The danger behind all these developments is that small-scale fighting can very quickly escalate into an all-out conflagration, with serious consequences for the Middle East and for the rest of the world.

Leading figures

Arafat, Yasser (1929–) leader of the PLO

Founder of *Fatah*, the largest of the Palestinian *fedayeen* groups, Yasser Arafat has become the living symbol of the Palestinian cause. Son of a wealthy Palestinian merchant based in Cairo and Gaza, Arafat studied as an engineer and was a successful businessman in Kuwait until the mid-1960s. He has been the PLO's chairman since 1969, and has survived countless Arab and Israeli attempts on his life (today he still reportedly never sleeps in the same place more than one night). In Palestinian terms, Arafat is a moderate: he publicly renounces terrorism, but justifies what he calls Palestinian resistance to Israeli rule inside Israel and the occupied territories, and he is prepared to negotiate peace on the basis of an independent Palestinian state in the occupied West Bank and Gaza Strip. He has the reputation of being a tireless worker, and incorrupt despite the vast financial resources at the PLO's disposal. His enemies accuse him of being untrustworthy and promising different things depending on whether he is addressing an Arab or a Western audience.

Lord Balfour (1848–1930) British foreign secretary 1916–19

Arthur James Balfour was born into an aristocratic family, and was elected a Conservative MP (Member of Parliament) at the age of twenty-six. He served as Chief Secretary for Ireland (where the Irish called him "Bloody Balfour" for his role in suppressing a nationalist revolt) before becoming prime minister in 1902. It was as foreign secretary during a World War I coalition government that he earned his most notable place in history, as the author of a letter in 1917 to Baron Rothschild, head of the English branch of the famous Jewish banking family. Later known as the Balfour Declaration, this letter promised support for Zionist efforts to establish a Jewish homeland in Palestine.

Begin, Menachem (1913–   ) Israeli prime minister

Begin was born in Poland, where his family suffered both Nazi and Soviet persecution. His parents and brother were killed in the Nazi Holocaust, and he himself was imprisoned in Siberia. He escaped to Palestine, where he took command of the Jewish underground movement, the *Irgun*, notorious for its acts of terrorism against both the British and the Arabs. Begin organized the blowing up of the King David Hotel in Jerusalem in 1946, and he commanded the group that massacred over 250 Arab villagers in Deir Yassin in 1948. At one point the British authorities had a £10,000 reward on his head. Begin was heavily influenced politically by the Zionist leader Jabotinsky (*q.v.*). Begin was first elected prime minister as leader of the right-wing Likud faction in 1977. His second government ordered the disastrous invasion of Lebanon in 1982, after which he resigned from office. Since then he has retired from political life.

Herzl, Theodor (1860–1904) founder of Zionism

Born in Budapest, Hungary, Herzl moved to Vienna as a child. His family were what are called assimilated Jews, that is, they were integrated into European society and did not practice their own religion. From his earliest days Herzl experienced the anti-Jewish racism then prevalent in Europe, but it was as a journalist covering the notorious Dreyfus affair that he became convinced anti-Semitism was inevitable in the Christian West, and that to escape persecution the Jews had to have a state of their own. (Dreyfus was a Jewish officer in the French army who was wrongly convicted in 1895 of treason.) Herzl's manifesto, *Der Judenstaat* (the State of the Jews), was published in 1896, and he went on to establish the World Zionist Organization in order to mobilize Jewish support for his idea.

Sharif Hussein and the Hashemites

Hussein ibn Ali (1856–1931) was reckoned thirty-seventh in line of descent from the Prophet Muhammad. He was a member of the Hashemite family of Arabia. In 1915 Sharif Hussein began exchanging letters with the British High Commissioner in Egypt, which led Hussein to believe that in return for launching a revolt against their Turkish rulers, Arabs of the Middle East would be given their independence. The Arab Revolt began in Mecca in June 1916, but the Hashemites gained little when they and the Allies defeated the Turks. One of Hussein's sons, Feisal, was briefly proclaimed King of Syria, but the French occupying army in Syria quickly threw him out. Embarrassed, the British installed Feisal as King of Iraq in 1921, although they remained the real power behind the Iraqi throne. Another of Hussein's sons, Abdullah, was installed as ruler of newly created Transjordan. Hussein himself was overthrown when the Saudis captured Mecca in 1924. Abdullah's grandson Hussein, ruler of what is today the Hashemite Kingdom of Jordan, has become the longest surviving Arab ruler.

Jabotinsky, Vladimir (1880–1940) Zionist leader

Jabotinsky was born in Czarist Russia, where he campaigned for the Jews to organize their own defense groups against the pogroms. In Palestine, Jabotinsky worked to organize armed Jewish groups to fight against the British and the Arabs. As early as 1916 he had become convinced that the Arabs had to be removed from Palestine in order to carry out the Zionist plan. In 1925 he said the establishment of a Jewish majority in Palestine would have to be achieved "against the will" of the country's Arab inhabitants. Jabotinsky founded the *Haganah,* the forerunner of today's Israeli army. Jabotinsky is remembered today as the founder of Revisionist Zionism, dedicated to the use of force as the way to expand Jewish control over Palestine.

Nasser, Gamal Abdel (1918–1970) Egyptian president

From a peasant background, Nasser was the first native Egyptian to rule the country for 2,500 years. Deeply resentful of Britain's occupation of Egypt, Nasser's whole life was dominated by struggle against foreign domination. His army career was the launching pad for his rise to power, and he assumed the presidency in 1954. The Suez Crisis of 1956 left Nasser the hero of Arab nationalism, but the popular expectations he raised could not be realized. Instead of Arab unity, divisions among the Arab states became deeper. Perhaps the worst blow to Nasser's vision of a united Arab world was the Jordanian-Palestinian civil war of 1970–71. Instead of "liberating Palestine" as he promised, Nasser led the Arab states to a disastrous defeat at the hands of Israel in 1967. He died suddenly in 1970, after mediating a ceasefire between King Hussein and the Palestinian *fedayeen.*

Sadat, Anwar (1918–1981) Egyptian president

The son of a government employee, Sadat graduated from Cairo's military academy in 1938. He took part in the 1952 Free Officers' coup, and held various posts in the new government. He was vice-president when Nasser died suddenly in 1970. Instead of the stopgap president many had expected, Sadat turned out to be a purposeful and powerful leader. At home he dismantled much of Nasser's socialism, and opened up the country to Western enterprise and investment. Abroad, he ended Egypt's close association with the USSR and embarked on an alliance with the United States. The military breakthrough he engineered against Israel in October 1973 could have made him the hero of the Arab world, but instead he went on to conclude a peace treaty with Israel, which the other Arab states denounced as a betrayal of the Arab cause. He became increasingly intolerant of opposition, and was assassinated in 1981.

Important dates

Date	Events
1878	First Zionist colony founded in Palestine.
1882	First large-scale Jewish immigration to Palestine.
1896	Herzl publishes *Der Judenstaat*.
1903	Second wave of Jewish immigration to Palestine.
1916	Sykes-Picot Agreement.
	Start of Arab Revolt, led by Hussein ibn Ali.
1917	Balfour Declaration.
	Ottoman forces in Jerusalem surrender to British army.
1919	Paris peace conference.
1920	Five Jews killed in riots in Palestine.
	San Remo Conference assigns Palestine Mandate to Britain.
1921	Jaffa Riots in Palestine.
1922	Transjordan excluded from Balfour Declaration.
1929	133 Jews, 116 Arabs killed in rioting in Jerusalem.
1935	*Irgun* formed.
1936	Palestine rebellion starts.
1937	British Peel Commission recommends partition of Palestine.
1939	British White Paper on Palestine.
	Palestine rebellion ends.
1946	King David Hotel in Jerusalem blown up by *Irgun*.
1947	Britain announces decision to end Palestine Mandate.
	UN General Assembly votes for partition of Palestine.
1948	Deir Yassin massacre.
	State of Israel proclaimed, British Mandate ends, Arab armies enter Palestine.
1949	Arab–Israeli Armistice Agreements.
1952	Free Officers coup in Egypt.
1956	Suez Crisis.
1964	PLO founded.
1967	*June* Six-Day War.
	November UN Security Council Resolution 242.
1968	Battle of Karameh.
1970	King Hussein attacks *fedayeen* in Jordan.
	Nasser dies.
1972	Sadat expels Soviet advisers from Egypt.
	Munich massacre of eleven Israeli Olympic athletes.
1973	October/Yom Kippur War.
	Arab oil boycott.
1974	First Sinai Disengagement Agreement.
	Arafat addresses UN General Assembly.
	Rabat Arab summit recognizes PLO.
1975	*April* Start of Lebanese civil war.
	September Second Sinai Disengagement Agreement.
	November UN General Assembly condemns Zionism as racist.

Date	Events
1977	Likud wins election in Israel.
	Joint U.S.–Soviet Declaration on Middle East peace.
	Sadat goes to Jerusalem to make a speech calling for peace.
1978	*March* Israel invades southern Lebanon.
	September Camp David talks in Maryland.
	November Baghdad Arab summit decides to isolate Egypt.
1979	Iranian Revolution.
	Egypt–Israel peace treaty signed.
1980	*June* EEC Venice Declaration on Middle East peace.
	September Gulf War starts.
1981	*June* Israel bombs Iraqi nuclear reactor.
	October Sadat assassinated by Muslim fundamentalists.
	December Israel annexes Syrian Golan Heights.
1982	*April* Israel returns last sector of occupied Sinai to Egypt.
	June Israel invades Lebanon, besieges Beirut.
	August PLO leave Lebanon.
	September Sabra/Chatila massacre.
1983	*August* Begin resigns as Israeli prime minister.
	October 241 U.S. Marines killed in Beirut suicide attack.
1984	*July* Israeli general election produces stalemate.
	September Likud-Labor coalition takes office in Israel.
1985	*June* Israel completes withdrawal from Lebanon.
1987	*December* Palestinian uprising in occupied territories begins.
1988	*November* Palestine National Council declares independent Palestinian state in occupied territories, accepts UN Resolution 242.
	December United States lifts ban on contacts with PLO.

Glossary

Annexation	Taking by one country of a piece of territory belonging to another.
Anti-Semitism	The Semitic peoples include both Arabs and Jews, but because Europeans were familiar only with Jews, in the West, anti-Semitism came to mean anti-Jewish racism.
Arab League	A league of independent Arab states formed in 1945, to further cultural, economic, military, political and social cooperation.
Arab nationalism	The political ideology shared by members of different states based on the principles of unity of all the Arab peoples and opposition to foreign domination.
Ashkenazi	Literally means German Jew. The common meaning is Jew of European origin, as opposed to *Sephardic* Jews from the Middle East.
Autonomy	Self-government.
Boycott	To refuse to deal with or trade with another state in order to force that state to abandon a position or action.
Democracy	Government by the people. A state in which its citizens have a free and equal right to vote for its government.
Demography	The science of population statistics. Israel's "demographic time bomb" refers to the fact that the Arab population has a higher birthrate than that of the Jewish population, and could in time outnumber the Jews in the State of Israel.
Diaspora	The scattering of a race or people around the world. Originally used of the Jews, it is also used today to describe the Palestinians.
EEC	European Economic Community. A group of West European countries that joined in a union to establish free trade.
Egalitarianism	The principle that all people should be equal – politically, socially and economically.
Eretz Yisrael	Literally means the "Land of Israel," a biblical term that right-wing Israelis take to include the occupied territories as well as Israel itself.
Exodus	Mass emigration of a people from a country. In particular, the biblical account of the flight of the Jews from Egypt in 1300 BC.
Haganah	Zionist militia that later grew into the Israeli army.
Holocaust	Devastation, especially by fire. In particular, the destruction of six million Jews by the Nazi government under orders from Hitler during World War II.
Ideology	A body of ideas that form a coherent system, often linked to a political plan, or way of thinking, that concerns social reform.
IDF	Israel Defense Force – the Israeli armed forces.
Invincible	Incapable of being defeated; unconquerable.
Irgun	The Jewish terrorist group inspired by Revisionist Zionism, disbanded in 1948.
Islam	The religion of Muslims; Muslims collectively and their civilization.
Islamic fundamentalism	A movement that aims to make the Muslim religion the dominant influence in politics, society, etc.
Israel	Biblically, the name given by God to Jacob, later meaning the Jewish people, and finally the name given to the Jewish state in 1948.

Kibbutz	The collective villages founded by early Zionists in Palestine, operating in principle without private property.
League of Nations	The international body established in 1919 with the aim of securing peace, justice and international cooperation. Superseded by the United Nations in 1945.
Mandate	The authority conferred on a country by the League of Nations to govern a former colony or occupied territory.
Marxism	The ideas of Karl Marx (1818–83), a German philosopher. He claimed to have discovered the laws that govern the behavior of human society in history: societies move from feudalism through capitalism to socialism, directed by economic forces. He held that most nineteenth-century states were in a capitalist phase and that revolution was needed to usher in the socialist (communist) era. For its believers, Marxism explains the present and offers hope for the future.
Orthodox Judaism	A strict form of the Jewish faith, demanding unfailing practice of personal devotions.
Ottoman Empire	The Turkish Muslim empire that ruled most of the Arab world from the sixteenth century to the start of the twentieth century.
PLO	Palestine Liberation Organization, founded in 1964, initially with the aim of creating a state for Palestinian Arabs and destroying the State of Israel.
Sephardic Jews	Jews from the Middle East, originally from Spain or Portugal. (See **Ashkenazi** above.)
Shi'ite	A member of a minority branch of Islam prevalent in Iran and southern Lebanon in particular. They reject Sunnite legal and political institutions.
Socialism	An economic theory that believes that the state should own all important means of the production and distribution of wealth.
Sunni	Mainstream Islam; the main branch of Islam.
Zionism	The political movement that worked for the establishment of the Jewish state. The word is derived from Mount Zion in Jerusalem.

Picture acknowledgments

The author and publishers would like to thank the following for allowing their illustrations to be reproduced in this book: BIPAC 7, 8, 12, 21 (top), 28, 35 (bottom), 38, 44; Camera Press cover, 17 (bottom), 31, 36, 37, 45 (top & bottom, John Tordai), 47 (Neil Libbert), 48 (John Tordai), 52 (bottom), 53; Michael Cummings, *Daily Express* 42; Emmwood, *Daily Mail* 33; Mary Evans 9, 10, 16; David Low, *Evening Standard* 21; Tony Stone 49; Topham 5 (left & right), 6, 11, 13, 15, 17 (top), 18, 19, 20, 23 (top), 24, 25, 26, 29 (top & bottom), 34, 35 (top), 40, 41, 43, 46, 51; UPI 50, 52 (top); Vicky, *Daily Mirror* 27; Keith Waite *The Sun* 30; Wayland 23 (bottom). Thanks also to the Centre for the Study of Cartoons and Caricature, University of Kent at Canterbury. The maps were supplied by Thames Cartographic Services Ltd.

Further reading

Text Books
Mansfield, Peter, *The Arabs*, Penguin, 1985.
Ruthven, Malise, *Islam in the World*, Oxford U. Press, 1984.
Sykes, Christopher, *Crossroads to Israel*, Indiana University Press, 1973.

Easier Books
Gilmour, David, *The Palestinians*,(gr. 4–9), Watts, 1986.
                     Lebanon the Fractured Country, St. Martin, 1984.
Hart, Alan, *Arafat: Terrorist or Peacemaker?*, Salem House Pubs., 1985.
Oz, Amos, *In the Land of Israel*, Random, 1984.
Rodinson, Maxime, *The Arabs*, U. of Chicago Press, 1981.
Shipler, David K., *Arab and Jew: Wounded Spirits in a Promised Land*, Penguin, 1987.
Turki, Fawaz, *The Disinherited: Journal of a Palestinian Exile*. Monthly Review Press, 1972.

Scholarly Works
Antonious, George,*The Arab Awakening*, International Book Center, 1976.
Chomsky, Noam, *The Fateful Triangle: The United States, Israel and the Palestinians*, South End Press, 1983.
Herzog, Chaim, *The Arab–Israeli Wars*. Random, 1982.
O'Brien, Conor Cruise, *The Siege: The Saga of Israel and Zionism*, Simon & Schuster, 1987.
Said, Edward, *The Question of Palestine*, Random, 1980.

Original Sources
Laqueur, Walter and Rubin, Barry M., *The Israeli–Arab Reader: A Documentary History of the Middle East Conflict*, Penguin, 1984.

Notes on sources

1 Laqueur, Walter and Rubin, Barry M., *The Israel–Arab Reader: A Documentary History of the Middle East Conflict*, Penguin, 1984.

2 *Ibid.*

3 *Ibid.*

4 Cited in Hirst, David, *The Gun and the Olive Branch*, Faber & Faber, 1977.

5 Berger, Elmer, *Who Knows Better Must Say So*, Institute for Palestine Studies, cited in Hirst, David, *The Gun and the Olive Branch*, Faber & Faber, 1977.

6 Guedalla, Philip, *Napoleon and Palestine.*

7 Memorandum to Lord Curzon, August 11, 1919. Cited in Ingrams, Doreen, *Seeds of Conflict*, John Murray, 1972.

8 O'Brien, Conor Cruise, *The Siege: The Saga of Israel and Zionism*, Simon and Schuster, 1987.

9 *Ibid.*

10 Turki, Fawaz, *The Disinherited: Journal of a Palestinian Exile*, Monthly Review Press, 1972.

11 Aruri, Nasser H., *The Middle East Crucible: Studies on the Arab–Israeli War of October 1973*, The Medina University Press International, 1975.

12 *Ibid.*

13 *Middle East International*, London, June 13, 1986.

14 Shipler, David K., *Arab and Jew: Wounded Spirits in a Promised Land*, Bloomsbury, 1987.

15 *Ibid.*

16 *The Observer*, London, October 30, 1988.

17 International Institute for Strategic Studies, London. Report issued October 1988.

Index

Figures in **bold** refer to illustrations.